Did You Learn To Love?

By Bonnie Jones

White Horses Publishing
Pineville, North Carolina

Did You Learn To Love?

Copyright © 2015 by Bonnie Jones

All rights reserved. No part of this book may be reproduced or transmitted in any form or by any means, electronic, mechanical, including photocopying, recording, or by any information storage and retrieval system, without written permission from White Horses Publishing.

Unless otherwise noted all Scripture quotations in the publication of "Did You Learn To Love?" are taken from the New King James Version. Copyright © 1982 by Thomas Nelson, Inc. Used by permission. All rights reserved.

Also Used the Amplified® Bible, Copyright © 1954, 1958, 1962, 1964, 1965, 1987 by the Lockman Foundation. Used by permission. (www.Lockman.org)

Cover art and book layout by Lyn Kost (704)-975-9631
lyn@bobjones.org

© 2015 Bonnie Jones

To obtain more of Bob Jones', Bonnie Jones' or Lyn Kost's written, video and audio teachings, prophecies and materials go to: www.BobJones.org

Or write to: White Horses Publishing
P.O. Box 838
Pineville, N.C. 28134-0838

Printed in the United States of America.
Produced & Distributed by White Horses Publishing

All rights reserved.

Dedication

I dedicate this book to the loving memory of my late husband and best friend Bob Jones. It was his greatest desire to reach the world with God's message, "Did you learn to Love?" Bob said, "It's the only question the Lord will ask when you stand before Him in death." Bob taught the body of Christ how to move in the gifts of the Spirit and understand the language of the Holy Spirit. In my opinion Bob was the greatest forerunner of the true prophetic movement. At a time when prophecy was greatly misunderstood, God brought forth His friend, Bob Jones, to mentor and form spiritual tools in the hand and heart of His emerging end-time army.

Bob and I planned to write and release this book for the fortieth anniversary of His death experience on August 8, 1975. Love is on the heart of the Father at all times and in all seasons. It is His divine nature and we are His offspring. Love is the only weapon the enemy has no defense against.

On behalf of the body of Christ, I thank Bob for his decision to return to earth that day in 1975. And for the years of persecution he endured in the process of bringing forth the prophetic movement. Without his sacrifice of love and patient endurance, the body of believers would be lacking in its spiritual understanding and weakened in its demonstration of power. Thank you, Bob Jones, for your sacrifice of love for the body. Thank you for your love for my family and myself. And most importantly, thank you for a never-ending love of the Father, Son and Holy Spirit. There's a debt of gratitude the body can never repay.

Acknowledgements

There are many people, both natural and spiritual, responsible for forming the life of Bob Jones into the man he became; a vessel of love transformed by the working of the Holy Spirit from within. To know Bob was to love him and receive the warmth and love of the Lord he generously expressed. I knew it would be a great undertaking to express Bob's death experience in book form and I would never been able to do it alone. Since Bob was no longer with us when I began writing I couldn't go back and ask more questions or his advice. I had to rely on our pre-recorded interview and memory. I'd like to take this time to honor those who willingly gave unselfishly of their time in the developing of "Did You Learn to Love?"

First, to my son Lyn Kost, thank you most of all for loving Bob as your father from the very beginning. He loved and honored you as his son and loved your sweet spirit and kind demeanor. Thank you for the endless hours of work you put into the formation of this book and artwork for the cover. You never got upset with me for making last minute changes and always helped me figure things out. Thank you for standing beside me in Bob's absence. You've grown in leaps and bounds in the Spirit as well as in the natural and I'm excited for all God is doing through you.

Next, to my daughter-in-law Katie Kost, thank you for loving Bob as your daddy and keeping him in line. You two were so comical to listen to as he teased you and your comebacks were outstanding. We always had lots of laughs. Thank you for giving

Bob his long awaited grandchildren; they brought him such joy. And personally let me say, "thank you" for transcribing the audiotape and editing the book. I know that was an incredible assignment but you did it splendidly and didn't change Bob's way of speaking Arkanese. Bless you!

And to my dear friend Marcia Rensink, thank you for being my friend through thick and thin without exception or expectation. You have been my one true constant. Thank you for taking time from your busy schedule to do the second edit on this book. It was through the eyes of love you encouraged me to stretch myself and look deeper into my heart. And you lovingly brought greater understanding to my gift and correction to my thought process. Bless you!

Finally, let me say a special "thank you" to everyone who wrote an endorsement for "Did You Learn to Love?" and Ricky Skaggs for writing the foreword. It was difficult to choose the right people for this task because Bob had so many beloved sons and daughters. I followed the leading of the Holy Spirit and He is never wrong. I want to thank each one of you for sharing your love, wisdom and personal insight not only regarding the book but more importantly for sharing your precious memories and love for Papa Bob. May God bless each of you abundantly!

Bonnie Jones

Endorsements

"It is an honor to endorse Bonnie's lovely book, a moving account of a most unique prophetic encounter of my special friend Bob Jones. Her book is full of her compassionate heart and wisdom. It is a tribute from a true spiritual friend. DID YOU LEARN TO LOVE? is sure to serve as an inspiration for you in-spiring you to deeper intimacy with Christ."

Bobby Conner
EaglesView Ministries
www.bobbyconner.org

"Bob touched millions of people with his life, and countless thousands testify that it was a word from him that set them on the course to fulfill their purpose. The main thing we heard from Bob the last few years of his life, and what is the most important message of Bob's life, Bonnie has captured in a very powerful way."

Rick Joyner
MorningStar Ministries
www.morningstarministries.org

"Many of us who were privileged to know Bob Jones have heard of his 1975 resurrection experience, and the promises that came out of it. However, we may never have heard the full story. Those who knew and appreciated Bob owe a debt of gratitude to Bonnie Jones and Lyn Kost for interviewing Bob before he died, and recording the entire episode in this book. It is a story that deserves to be repeated. It is a story that must be repeated by all those who are learning to love."

Randal Cutter
New Dawn Community Church
www.newdawn.org

"Bob Jones has been and will always be my friend, a mentor, much more than a teacher, and he was like a father to me. For more than 30 years I closely watched Bob Jones grow, live and impart this all important message of love, and I will be forever grateful.

This book is about a man who was like a second father to me; everything I know is because of him. Bob's words have always called me to greatness. He taught me how special the love of friendship was by being a friend to me and to Jesus. Like Peter when he was asked three times if he loved Jesus, affirmed from his heart his friendship each time and then received his commission to feed others with this love. A true friend is someone who knows all about you believes in you and still loves you. This is one of the greatest lessons I have received from the life of Bob and Bonnie Jones, and I could not love anybody more."

Bob Hartley
Deeper Waters
www.bobhartley.com

"Bonnie Jones is one of the most gifted prophetic leaders of our day. She carries a powerful anointing and draws from a deep well of wisdom and insight because of her passionate walk with Christ that has spanned decades. Within the pages of "Did You

Learn To Love?" we are given a rare glimpse into the life of her late husband, Bob Jones, a true friend of God and one of the greatest prophetic voices over the past century. This extraordi-nary book is a remarkable treasure that reveals Bob's life-mes-sage of love and is imperative for every believer to be transformed as a vessel of love during their walk on earth. It is a must read. From the many years I have spent as a close friend to Bob and Bonnie, I can say that Bonnie models the very essence of the compassion and love she writes about. There has never been a greater need than now for this message to be her- alded to the world. It gives us a much needed view into the very heart of God and carries the power to manifest God's love throughout the world."

Gary Beaton
Transformation Glory Ministries
www.transformationglory.com

"For many years I had the great honor and privilege of doing life with Bob Jones. The love that he shared and poured into me changed me and played a big part in making me who I am today. Many people may have many different things to say about Bob Jones, but from my years with him, I knew him to be one of the most powerful, authentic, love filled people I've ever known. I miss him greatly. His life and legacy made and is making an im- pact on multitudes of people because he truly lived out the life message of this book "Did you learn to love?" I believe that if every follower of Jesus could make it the aim of their life to sim- ply learn to love with the same radical love that Jesus gave to the world…this world would never be the same! This was the dream of Bob's heart and it's the dream on God's heart. You and

I now carry the baton. Let's make our lives count. Let's learn to love. Let's change the world!"

Ryan Wyatt
Fuse Church
www.fusechurch.com

"When I read through this book I was consumed by the Holy Spirit all the time as waves of love flooded me. This is a must read for all the body of Christ. This is a true reflection of what love really is and should be. What makes it so powerful is that it comes out of a testimony, power, of a man that lived and experienced it himself. This book will create a desire in everyone to move back into a realm of perfect love. This will advance your perception of love and how to restore Father on the throne of First Love. When God is your first love, love becomes a reality and lifestyle.

I honour Bob Jones for the example he gave the body of Christ and for all the sacrifices. This is a excellent book and true reflection by Bonnie in partnership with the Holy Spirit."

Etienne Blom
Kingdom Fire Ministries
www.kingdomfire.ca

"Bonnie and Lyn have skillfully captured the essence of Bob Jones' ministry in "Did You Learn to Love?" However, this won-derful book is much more than a story about Bob's encounter with God's heart for humanity. It is a testimony to the "power of love" through the life of a man who rarely missed an oppor-tunity to encourage everyone he met.

As Bob's friend of many years, I personally know what it feels like to experience heaven's unconditional love and acceptance through another human being. Honestly, of all the things I so terribly miss about Bob was the knowing twinkle in his eye and the kind expression of God's smile, often present on his face. This memory is and will forever be alive deep within my heart. Thank you Bob for "Did You Learn to Love?"

Larry Randolph
Larry Randolph Ministries
www.larryrandolph.com

Foreword

THE SCRIPTURES TELL US IN 1 CORINTHIANS 4:15, "THOUGH YOU HAVE MANY INSTRUCTORS IN CHRIST, YOU HAVE SO FEW FATHERS: FOR IN CHRIST JESUS I HAVE BEGOTTEN YOU THROUGH THE GOSPEL." THAT WAS WHAT BOB JONES DID SO WELL. HE FATHERED US THROUGH THE GOSPEL AND CALLED US UP HIGHER INTO THE HEAVENLY REALM WHERE HIS PAPA LIVES. HE CALLED THE FATHER "PAPA" BECAUSE JESUS CALLED HIM ABBA, WHICH IS PAPA. HE ALWAYS WANTED TO DO THE THINGS THAT JESUS DID. BOB TAUGHT ON THE ORPHAN SPIRIT THAT WE ARE ALL BORN INTO. IT WAS ADAM'S SIN IN THE GARDEN THAT SEPARATED US FROM GOD. HE CALLED THAT SIN THE OLD NATURE. HE KNEW THAT WHEN HE GOT SAVED, HE WASN'T AN ORPHAN ANYMORE. HE KNEW THAT HIS HEAVENLY PAPA HAD ADOPTED HIM, AND HE ALSO BELIEVED THAT HE WOULD NEVER GET KICKED OUT OF THE FAMILY. ALTHOUGH HE GOT GET KICKED OUT OF A FEW CHURCHES, HE WORE THOSE SCARS AS BADGES OF HONOUR.

MANY CALLED BOB A GREAT PROPHET, AND HE WAS, OTHERS SAID HE WAS A SEER, AND YES HE SAW. THERE WERE MANY MIRACLES, MANY HEALINGS, AND MANY SOULS SAVED AT HIS MEETINGS, BUT IF YOU ASKED BOB WHAT WAS THE GREATEST THING THAT CHRIST EVER DID FOR HIM, BESIDES DYING ON THE CROSS, HE WOULDN'T POINT TO THE

MIRACLES OR THE DREAMS THAT HE HAD, OR THE ANGELS THAT HE SAW, OR THE PROPHETIC WORDS THAT HE HAD GIVEN SOMEONE, HE WOULD ALWAYS SAY, "HE TAUGHT ME HOW TO LOVE." SO IN MY HEART, BOB WAS A PROPHET OF LOVE.

WHEN I WOULD ASK HIM A QUESTION ABOUT SOMETHING SPIRITUAL, HE WOULD ALWAYS SAY, "IT'S IN THE BIBLE, YOU OUGHT TO FIND IT AND LOOK IT OVER." AND SURE ENEOUGH, I'D FIND IT EVENTUALLY. HE WASN'T BEING MEAN, HE WAS JUST BEING A GOOD DADDY TEACHING HIS KIDS HOW TO BELIEVE FOR THEMSELVES. ONE TIME HE SHOWED ME PROVERBS 25:2, 'IT IS THE GLORY OF GOD TO CONCEAL A THING, BUT THE HONOUR OF KINGS IS TO SEARCH OUT A MATTER.' HE SAID, "THAT'S WHY I WANT YOU TO SEARCH THESE THINGS OUT, SO YOU'LL KNOW WHERE THEY ARE. YOU WON'T ALWAYS HAVE ME AROUND.

I DON'T WANNA RAISE UP CRIPPLE'S TO DEPENDING ON ME. YOU HAVE TO LEARN HOW TO WALK ON YOUR OWN AND DO THESE THINGS YOURSELF. ANYTHING THAT JESUS DID, WE CAN DO TOO. THAT'S WHY HE LEFT HERE AND WENT TO HEAVEN. HE DID HIS PART, AND HE GIVE US HIS AUTHORITY.

TO DO GREATER THINGS THAN HE DID. IF YOU'RE GONNA DO THE GREATER WORKS, YOU'RE GONNA HAVE TO HAVE THE GREATER LOVE." THOSE WORDS

WAS A LITTLE HARD FOR ME TO UNDERSTAND WHEN I WAS FIRST GETTING TO KNOW BOB, BUT THE MORE I DID WHAT HE TOLD ME TO DO, THE MORE I UNDERSTOOD THAT HE SAID THOSE THINGS BECAUSE HE LOVED ME AND WANTED THE BEST FOR ME.

AS I READ THIS BOOK "DID YOU LEARN TO LOVE?" THAT BOB'S PRECIOUS WIFE AND SWEETHEART BONNIE JONES HAS WRITTEN, IT BROUGHT BACK SO MANY GREAT MEMORIES. FOR ALL OF YOU THAT WAS BLESSED TO KNOW BOB AND HIS MINISTRY, YOU MIGHT HAVE HEARD A FEW OF THESE STORIES, BUT THROUGH THE EYES, EARS AND HEART OF BONNIE, THEY WILL BECOME FRESH AND NEW AGAIN. THE WONDERFUL OPENING, WHICH IS AN INTERVIEW WITH BOB, IS PRICELESS. I'VE HEARD THE STORY OF HIM GOING TO HEAVEN IN DEATH BACK IN 1975 FOR PREACHING AGAINST THE THREE SIN'S IN AMERICA, BUT I HADN'T HEARD IT WITH THE CLAIRITY THAT HE TELLS BONNIE SITTING IN THEIR LIVING ROOM. I PROMISE, THIS WILL BLESS YOU AND GIVE YOU A WHOLE NEW PERSPECTIVE ON HEAVEN, ON THE LOST, AND HOW THE FATHERS' HEART GRIEVES FOR THEM, AND HOW WE SHOULD GRIEVE FOR THEM TOO. BONNIE ALSO TEACHES ON MANY OF THE THINGS THAT SHE'S LEARNED FROM BOB, BUT ALSO HOW SHE'S HAD TO LEARN THESE THINGS ON HER OWN THROUGH THE HOLY SPIRIT.

BONNIE, I KNOW THAT BOB IS SO PROUD OF YOU AND

THE WAY THAT YOU'VE HONORED HIM, BUT MOST IMPORTANTLY HOW YOU'VE HONORED THE ONE WHO DESERVES ALL HONOR AND GLORY, OUR PRECIOUS KING AND LORD, JESUS CHRIST. WELL DONE DEAR SISTER!

THERE ARE MANY PEOPLE IN THIS WORLD THAT KNEW BOB BETTER THAN I DID, AND THEY COULD HAVE DONE A MUCH BETTER JOB WRITING THIS FORWARD, BUT THERE IS NO ONE THAT IS MORE GRATEFUL TO THE LORD FOR BEING ASKED TO DO THIS THAN ME. I HOPE AND PRAY THAT WHEN I STAND BEFORE THE LORD ONE DAY AND HE ASKS ME, "DID YOU LEARN TO LOVE?" I CAN SAY WITH ALL THAT IS WITHIN ME "YES LORD, BECAUSE OF YOU I LEARNED TO LOVE." THANK YOU JESUS AND BOB JONES.

Ricky Skaggs

Table of Contents

I.	THE APPARITION	1
II.	TWO DISTINCT LINES	19
III.	RETURN FROM DEATH	33
IV.	HOW CAN I LEARN TO LOVE	49
V.	LOVE IS THE UNIVERSAL KEY	59
VI.	PREFERRING OTHERS FIRST	67
VII.	CREATED IN HIS LOVE	73
	PHOTO GALLERY	83

Love is the universal language that declares the Truth. Its voice is as soft as a whisper and gentle as a breeze. Its breath carries the authority of a Lion yet it speaks gentle as a Lamb. Its tears are full of compassion that heals the wounds of the heart. From conception till death it feeds the spirit and never shall depart. Long after death, Love is remembered in the hearts of those it knew. Love is a sweet remembrance and a gift to me and you.

I

THE APPARITION

*The Power of Love is Sweet.
Its Fragrance is Strong.
Its Armor is Unbeatable.*

The Apparition

The beginning of this book is taken directly from an in depth interview with Bob Jones from 2010. I felt it was important to keep it as near to the original story as possible. Many people have heard Bob recount his death experience and over the years we've gleaned the most important parts, such as the question "did you learn to love?" the billion soul harvest and the return of the glory. However, there is much more to this story and I'd like to share it with you. I hope you can hear Bob's voice as you read it.

On the day of this interview Bob, my son and I were relaxing in the living room. I had just prepared dinner and placed Cornish hens in the oven before we began. I planned plenty of time for the interview and a reward for the starving prophet when he finished. If you knew Bob, you know he liked to eat. You will enjoy his comment at the end of the interview.

As Bob recounts his death experience from 1975, he begins by giving us details from Wednesday, August 6, 1975. He was driving his blue pick-up truck; Viola and their dog were with him. They had just left their farm on the Lake of the Ozarks and were heading toward home in Independence, Missouri. They were traveling on a major highway - I 65.

The interview begins:

Bonnie: Now I'm just trying to get some details. Where were you? Were you in the city or out in the country?

Bob: At a farm down in the Lake of the Ozarks.

Bonnie: Oh, you were at your farm.

Bob: No, I was at my farm coming back to my house. I was on the highway.

Bonnie: So it was a country road maybe?

Bob: No it was a major highway. 65 Highway.

Bonnie: Did you stop driving?

Bob: Nope. I kept driving.

Bonnie: So the light came in and you just heard the voice then?

Bob: Yep. The voice started talking to me.

Bonnie: Did you answer or anything?

Bob: No I listened. How would you answer a thing like that?

Bonnie: Well, I don't know.

Bob: I didn't have any answers. So He spoke of the three major sins that would overtake America.

Bonnie: The Lord had given you some messages and that's why the devil killed you? The three things were homosexuality,

Bob: Yep and abortion and drugs.

Bonnie: Ok, so those were the three. How did the Lord bring those messages to you? Did He bring them to you all at one time?

Bob: Yes, all at one time. I was riding in a pick-up and a white light, about the size of a basketball, comes in to where I was.

Bonnie: So, did Viola see the light come in too?

Bob: Uh, no she didn't see it.

The Three Sins
1. Homosexual Disease

Bob: All of a sudden a white light, about the size of a basketball, came into the truck where I was. A voice came out of the white light like a sun, and He began to speak to me. He began to tell me about abortion and said that homosexuals were going to come out of the closet because at that time they were still in the closet. He said the homosexuals were going to demonstrate in the streets and in the capitol of this nation. And literally they would make it like homosexuality was normal. He said that there would be a judgment come upon them. It was a virus that couldn't be healed and He called it a homosexual disease. He said, "Tell them that if they don't want this disease then don't have any part of the sin." He said that five million homosexuals would be dying of this disease by the year 2000 and they would double year by year after that until they begin to repent on this sin.

I didn't know it then but the homosexual disease that could not be cured is AIDS.

2. Abortion

Then He said, "They're going to begin to perfect abortion on a scale that's never been heard of before." He said that the last stages of abortion would be a pill and it would be invented by the devil. They would call it an abortion pill and women would take it and it would abort the child. And what it would do to the child, it would push or disconnect the child away from the womb and the child would literally die by starvation. He said, "Every one of these things that they do I will bring a judgment against it." And as it pushed the baby away from the wall to starve it He would push the nation back from Him and starve them. Every way that they killed these unborn children is a judgment that will come on the nation.

"They will perfect abortion according to the gods that were worshipped in ancient Israel." One of them would be like the god Molech where they threw a baby into the red-hot idol's arms and burned it alive. That's the saline solution. Then He said, "Many people for convenience will literally fillet their own baby as they did in the Old Testament where they ate their own children. It's when they take the baby out piece by piece."

I didn't have any answers. So He spoke of the three major sins that would overtake America.

3. Meth Labs

He said, "There would be two cheap chemicals and that by mixing them together would become a narcotic and it would destroy people's conscience. They would not be conscious of sin. And as they took this drug they wouldn't even be under conviction for their sins. They would be totally heartless." And that was the meth labs and they did grow worse and worse.

Bonnie: Did you know at that time that He was talking about meth labs?

Bob: No I didn't have any idea. He said two cheap chemicals. I had no idea what they were. But I did bring that word over and over before meth labs even came into existence. This meth lab would also bring sores upon them because it would begin to destroy their natural body and their immunity.

Bonnie: Is that something that He told you?

Bob: Yeah, yeah, I saw that it would look like they had a fatal disease. And they did. And these meth labs, I think the fatal disease not only goes into them but into their children. I think it would damage the chromosomes to where children would be born without a natural conviction rendering them heartless. He said that the pressure would become so great on the United States that free drugs would be issued to calm people down. It already is to a degree now.

Bonnie: So you're just talking about the United States?

Bob: I'm talking about the whole world. But the United States has been a big exporter of it. Our sin is greater because we export it.

Bonnie: So you're saying there would be a judgment for all three, the meth labs, abortion, and homosexuality? But with the abortion did you say that there would be a…

Bob: Abortion would bring a judgment that would come because abortion is a convenience. Well, exactly opposite would come because of the abortion…it would be an inconvenience. Women that have had abortions, as they grow a little older they'll have nothing. They'll have no children to help feed them or anything else. They'll literally starve for affection and everything else because of their evil sins and their self-centeredness. They had an abortion for convenience. They chose a job and prestige over children. Therefore as they grow older they will not have any children or prestige or a job. And this will be a judgment against them. For every abortion that they have will scar their heart more and more.

Lyn: When He came into the truck as a Light, did He speak to you? Was it an instantaneous word where you knew everything all at once or did it take a couple of minutes while you were driving?

Bob: I would say it took ten minutes or better as my mind could get it. And I knew that voice that was coming out of that big white light, like the sun. I didn't know whether it was the Holy Spirit or Jesus. But what difference would that make? It was still

God. I believe it was Jesus. And this was really grieving His heart, all of these sins.

Judgment

Bob comments: But at the time they issue this abortion drug, this pill, it's a time this nation will know judgment. I think they call it UR 486 or something like that. It's the abortion pill. And they haven't yet really released it in the United States. They have in other nations and you can get it in the United States.

Bonnie: In the nations where it's already been released, have they come under judgment?

Bob: Well, all the nations are under judgment right now. Ours is the greatest sin because we exported the technology on how to do it, and we've supported it. We've supported abortion and therefore many things for us are being aborted. And the main thing on this is - if you don't want to be part of the judgment then don't be part of the sin. Stay out of homosexuality. Stay out of abortions. Stay out of drugs. So He spoke these things to me in my pick-up truck and then left.

Demonic Visitation

I drove us home and the next night we were meeting with some people in a church. I brought these prophecies and after church that night a demon appeared to me. The demon appeared to me on the night of August 7th and said, "If you share those prophecies anymore I will kill you! Go on and do your healings and everything else and I'll leave you alone."

Bonnie: Ok, so it's August 7th when you went to church (*Bob confirms*) and you shared these prophecies. How did the people at the church respond? Was it a big church or small church?

Bob: Pretty good-sized church. (*Bob gives name of church and denomination but asks it not be written down.*)

Bonnie: Ok, well, how did the people respond when you brought these prophecies? Were they in shock at such a thing?

Bob: No, they didn't believe me.

Bonnie: So they were unbelieving.

Bob: They said that in 1975 that couldn't possibly happen anywhere.

Bonnie: So they were in unbelief?

Bob: They didn't believe it at all. And so, that night this demon spoke to me and said, "Don't ever share that again. If you do I'll kill you!" And I wasn't the least concerned cause I wasn't his property. And neither did I believe that he could kill me in anyway.

Lyn: Did he show up in your house?

Bob: He showed up in a trance when I was in my bed. I was in a trance that night and a spirit of death came in, which is a demon. He threatened me. On the morning of August 8th people called me about this prophecy and I began to share it with them again. The demon said I could do the healings and prophesy and everything else and he'd leave me alone. "Just don't prophesy this!" He said not to share what the white light told me.

Bonnie: Did you have conversation with him then?

Bob: I literally said, "I'm not your property. I'm not afraid of you. I don't belong to you!"

Bonnie: And what did he say?

Bob: Nothing! He was gone. So, on the morning of August the 8th of 1975, I got up in the morning. And after taking several phone calls from church people about this prophecy, I left for work. I was doing tree work and we went that day to top a tree.

Bonnie: Oh, okay, so that was actually on the 8th when people from the church started calling? What kind of questions did they ask you?

Bob: Well, they were saying, "Would you repeat the prophecy? How did you hear it?" In other words they were really questioning me. So I repeated the prophecy. And I think I repeated it three or four times that morning before I went to work. And see, I was warned to not share it with them anymore. But I did share it that morning with different ones from nine o'clock till ten or eleven o'clock and then we went out to work.

Bonnie: Who are "we"?

Bob: My son Wayne and I. And we got out there and I did a job and I was beginning to do another one when all of a sudden I was hit with pain around my belt. It just literally nearly took the breath out of me. I just came out of a tree; it wasn't a big tree. It was a smaller tree and we were spraying too. And it hurt me so bad that I couldn't drive. Wayne drove me home. I was in such bad shape that Viola said, "Load him up, we need to take him the doctor."

Lyn: I was just going to ask if, when you started to feel the pain or right around that time, did you see anything or hear anything? Or were you just experiencing the physical?

Bob: Nope, I mean it was just horrible. One minute natural, the next minute one of the most horrible pains I've ever known.

Bonnie: I've heard you say this before about the pain, was it in your stomach?

Bob: Right from my belt down.

Bonnie: But the pain was actually in your stomach, right?

Bob: Yeah, in my lower stomach, below the belt. And it got as hard as a rock. I've heard many doctors say different things. I don't really know what it was. I've heard them say many things like: if it came that way people never recover once major things in your body explode like that. What do you call it the main…

Bonnie: Artery?

Bob: Yeah, I mean the main one.

Bonnie: Was it an aneurysm?

Bob: Well, I don't know what it was, but they said…see you got main arteries in your legs…

Bonnie: Femoral arteries.

Bob: Yeah, I forget what they're called. But if that blows out then you start bleeding. And if you don't get to the doctor's you're not going to last long. So we went to the house. Viola loaded me up and Wayne drove us to the doctor's office. The doctor said "We'd better get him into the hospital. I've never seen anything like this and I don't know what it is, but he's in bad shape."

I thought, "Oh! Now, I understand it. This is what the devil is doing and I'm not his property." And the doctor said, "It's serious!" And I said "If it's serious and I'm gonna die I want to die in my own bed. Take me home." So he gives me some pain pills and I went home and took the first pain pill. Five minutes later the pain was so intense, the pill didn't touch it at all. I took the second pain pill. Five minutes later it hadn't affected it at all. So I took the third pain pill. When I did, blood began to come out of my mouth like a geyser. I could see some of the pain pills broken up but they hadn't even dissolved yet. And the pain was so great…I was too weak to scream.

Bonnie: Was anybody in the room with you then or not?

Bob: Well, Wayne and Viola was.

Bonnie: When you started bleeding from the mouth?

Bob: Uh, no I run 'em out.

Bonnie: OK, so you were in there by yourself?

Bob: Well, I got a wet towel and wrapped it around my head. I thought Lord, "This is serious!" I was keeping the blood off the bed.

Bonnie: OK so you wrapped the wet towel around your forehead?

Bob: Yeah I just wrapped it around my head (like a scarf) to where the blood was going into the towel. Well, I wrapped it all the way around my head but it was covering my mouth. It was wet.

Bonnie: Bringing clarity, you went to the doctor's office and the doctor said he hadn't seen anything like that and they should take you to the hospital. But that's when you said "No, I want to go home." Correct?

Bob: Yes, cause, it was demonic. What could they do for you in the hospital? So I've had kidney stones and they are really painful. They tell me the kidney stone is like the pain of childbirth, about equal. This was far beyond that. The pain was so bad that it made you so weak you couldn't do anything. I didn't even have enough strength in me to scream.

Bonnie: What time of day did this attack start?

Bob: I think it started right at noon and blood started coming out my mouth at three o'clock.

The Cave

Bob: So about three o'clock that evening the pain was so severe that I was praying to pass out. Then, all of a sudden, the pain stopped and I was in a dark cave. I looked down there, I'd say about a hundred yards at the face of that cave, and there was sunlight. It was like the sun itself only there was a man. The sunlight was really bright but there was a man inside that sunlight who was brighter. That man had the most beautiful blue eyes I've ever seen. I was about a hundred yards from Him but I could see His eyes from there.

All of a sudden I thought, "I haven't made it. I have died." As I was sitting there like that I began to think, "Oh, have I spotted my robe? Is this why I was killed? Is there sin in my life that I was killed for? Have I come home with a spot on my robe?" There was a man there that was also black light whose face I couldn't see because it was too bright of light that I couldn't look into it. But I had known Him before and He stood by me many times.

When I first got acquainted with Him He really scared me bad.

He scared me to where, at different times, I was hoping He'd never show up again. But this time He was standing there and I looked where that light was. He said, "Now Bob, you can look and see." So I looked at myself and I could see a white linen robe that just shone. It had inner glory in it that was awesome. I looked at it and I was so shocked for there weren't any spots on it. And He said, "Are you ready to begin your walk?" I said, "Yeah!" So we began to walk and the closer we got to that light I began to think, "This is the greatest day that I've ever lived."

Bonnie: So you're in the cave as you call it and you can see the white light a hundred yards ahead of you?

Bob: Well, that cave was a like a portal, honey.

Bonnie: Well, I've heard other people call it a tunnel.

Bob: Yeah, a tunnel. A tunnel is right or a portal.

Lyn: Is it facing straight?

Bob: It was straight. There was no bumps, no nothing; just a straight easy walk.

Lyn: OK, so it was horizontal then?

Bob: Totally horizontal.

Bonnie: OK but you're here and in the distance you can see the white light and you can see His eyes?

Bob: Yeah, a hundred yards. Those eyes; they didn't have any depth to them.

Bonnie: Was that the Lord that you were seeing?

Bob: Yes.

Bonnie: And the Holy Spirit was beside you?

Bob: Yes, the Paraclete was walking beside me. And that's what He does. Paraclete means the one that walks by your side. And He was walking by my side explaining things to me. So we walked down the mouth of that tunnel and as I stepped out something fell on me. It was like a joy that I've never known before. And it just fell all over me. I was just wrapped up like a cocoon in it. I said, "What is this joy?" He said, "It's the love of God that has fallen on you. And I was thinking, "It's so bright." And He said, "Yeah, that's the glory of God." So the love and the glory are really like a cocoon and I was wrapped up in it.

If I take all of the good feelings I've ever had in life and multiply it a million times, it wouldn't even come close to touching how well I felt. I felt totally loved. I felt the glory of God just surround me like a blanket of love, a cocoon of love. So I asked the Man that stood beside me, "What is this?" He said, "It's the love of God." And I said, "This light is the love too?" He said, "No, the light is the glory." And I said, "How can it be both?" He said, "John 17, the glory and the love I had with the Father in the beginning." So John 17 is one powerful book. Then I stepped out into the light and I saw a line leading to the Man with the blue eyes.

Bonnie: OK, so now you're out of the tunnel?

II
TWO DISTINCT LINES

Love is an open door to access the Father.
Love is an everlasting smile of approval.
It's the road less traveled - yet love is the lonely mile.
Love is the unclaimed baggage left behind.

The Forsaken

Bob: Yes, I'm out of the tunnel and I see this line and there were people in the line that I was in. Then the Paraclete said, "Look to your left." And I looked to my left and for each two people that were in my line there were ninety-eight people in the other line. Only the people in the other line couldn't walk. They were wrapped up in the gods they served on the earth. So the faceless man began to show me. He said, "This was his god. He's going into death with his god and through all eternity he will be with his god." And I looked at them and I saw them as they began to look and see that sunlight in those eyes. Each one's eyes got big and their mouth's dropped. You could see them saying, "He is real. We mocked and we laughed but He is real."

Did you ever see rollers in the supermarket where they roll boxes on them? Well, these people were on rollers. They had no control they were being rolled right up there.

Bonnie: I've heard you say that a lot of times. When you came out of that tunnel and into the light you were in the line on the right side, correct?

Bob: Yes, on the right side.

Bonnie: And the Holy Spirit says to look over there, to those that are over there…

Bob: Yeah, on the left side.

Bonnie: So you did, but you said, "They looked…and they said, "He's real and we mocked Him and we laughed at Him." So were they looking over to your line and seeing Jesus?

Bob: No, they were looking to the Sunlight.

Bonnie: OK so the Sunlight….

Bob: The second they came out of that cave they saw Him. They came out of a different tunnel than I did. But the moment they came out they saw Him, I mean we all saw Him!

Bonnie: That's what I was trying to figure out, where He was. Was He in the middle between the two lines?

Bob: Ah no. He was on my side.

Bonnie: OK.

Bob: It was like immediately when they come out of the tunnel they understood all things. I mean it was like they understood the Truth. I saw them roll up there and they looked at Him. Then it was like the rollers went down. And as they went down I saw that all of it was like a dark darkness. Through all eternity they will be with their god in that darkness. They'll never see the light of God again. Everyone from all kindred and tongues…everything in different ways speaks of God. So they all had the witness that God was a Spirit. They had to witness it, that He was God.

Bonnie: OK. So you're here on the right side and there are ones on the left that the Holy Spirit tells you to look at. (Bob confirms) And you see them on rollers and they have understanding. Now, does your focus remain there or does it come back here to your line?

Bob: My focus was like I was paralyzed watching that line.

Bonnie: OK so your focus is then on what's going on over there.

Bob: Ooh, that focus was horrible. That line was so horrible.

Bonnie: Try to remember everything that you saw over there.

Bob: Well, one of the first things I saw was a man wrapped up in sod because his yard had been his god. He was wrapped up in sod like a mummy. He couldn't move, he could talk and he couldn't do anything. The sod was his god. He rolled up there and down into that tunnel he went. I saw another man, and women too, whose heads where sticking out of a whiskey bottle.

Bonnie: So there's more than one?

Bob: Oh yeah many, many because alcohol was their god. I saw men and women with needles jabbing themselves just over and over trying to get a fix but all it did was like burning acid going into them. Well, it was horrible! And they would keep shooting that stuff into them because drugs had been their god.

I saw a man that had died in lust and that spirit of lust had been his god. He would go into eternity with it never being able to touch it and it would torment him day and night. He'd never get any satisfaction out of it. It would be like a hot fire on him day and night.

And then I saw a really horrible thing. Can you imagine a thousand pound pumpkin? It was just a man's head…the pumpkin was. Every time I would see these things the Holy Spirit would explain what it was. I was waiting for Him to explain this and He said, "This man is an atheist. He said that he didn't worship any god but he did. He worshiped himself. And in eternity all he'll be is one head, nothing else! For all eternity he'll have just one tormenting thought after another because he was an atheist. Therefore he did have a god, it was himself, and he'll be in prison for all time with himself."

Then I was told that this isn't for a thousand or a hundred thousand years. This is for eternity. This will never end for them. I didn't see the lake of fire or anything else like that. I just saw darkness beyond imagination.

Bonnie: Wasn't there a man with money?

Bob: Yeah well the man with money was wrapped up in dollar-bills, honey. He was wrapped in dollar bills so money was his god. And he'd spend eternity wrapped up in dollars bills but he could never spend a one. They had him imprisoned. There would be no movement there. He couldn't even move his head. He was like a mummy that had been wrapped up alive. And it was like he would spend all of his eternity wrapped up there. It's like his clothing was dollar bills. Money was his god.

Bonnie: Were there other ones that you saw over there?

Bob: Uh, yeah I saw many, but I really can't remember that many right now. I did remember their eyes though. So every god down here that man worships or follows instead of Jesus is the god he'll serve in Hell forever. That cave they went into was so dark that I could see it was a Hell beyond man's understanding. I felt that one of the worst parts of that Hell was there would never be a light again. Never would the Son's light shine on them again. Theirs was an eternal torment - day and night for all eternity.

Our lives here are fifty to a hundred years and it determines where we will spend eternity. We go through some testing but this is nothing to what they go through; for ours is usually less than a hundred years but theirs is eon after eon after eon after eon of screaming and hollering. And whichever god they worshipped here is the god they'll spend eternity with. I was getting sick to be honest with you and I turned my head away from it.

The Righteous

Then I saw people in a line that was in front of me. As the line got closer and closer to the light I began to hear Him speak one thing to each one of them. I saw a black woman that was around probably six foot tall and around three hundred pounds. She had over a hundred angels with her. So I asked the faceless man, "Why so many angels?" He said, "She was a great evangelist and a great mother in her time. It's her time and she's going home." I watched as she came close to Him. He asked her one question. It was like, "Daughter, did you learn to love?" And she threw her hands up and said, "Oh, yes Lord I learned to love!" Then He kissed her on the lips and double doors opened up in His heart. He put His arms around her and in she went right into His heart, and all those angels with her.

I asked the faceless man, "Why are they going home with her?" He said, "Because they helped her do ministry on the earth and they're going home with her. You see, you're going to judge angels. And the judging you'll do is how much they helped you do things." For angels have no testimony. They have a testimony when they help a saint do something. So when they go home they'll have that testimony in heaven. And that's where we'll judge angels, by what they help us do. In other words we'll confirm that they were part of what we did. They will be equal partakers in what we did. Also everybody that is praying for these ministries, these awesome ministers and what they did. I saw the people that were never seen out in the open were equal partakers with that black sister. For see they'd supported her and they prayed for her. So what she did, they had a testimony beyond anything they imagined.

It was already laid up for them. They gave it in their gifts and their intercession. So many of these hidden ministries are how the church keeps moving. I call it the ministry of helps. The ministry of helps is like grease that keeps the machinery of the church moving. Without ministry of helps the church will break down and burn out. The very best ministries of helps are hidden.

The second one I saw in the line was a little girl about eleven years old. She had the most beautiful ministry of helps as I've ever seen. I was told that she had become crippled at five years old and bedfast shortly after that. She lay bedfast and prayed day and night for the saints and she was going home in the condition she died with. I said, "Why isn't she straightened up?" The Paraclete said, "This is her testimony. In heaven she's going to walk around this way at different times to show the people how much opposition she had and how she broke through."

Bonnie: So while the little girl is in line, she's still crippled?

Bob: Yup! She wouldn't be when she went into Him but at different times her testimony in heaven will be, "Here's how I was." You've got to understand, Heaven is a place of testimonies.

Bonnie: That's how I was thinking, like my mom; she could go to heaven being all crippled up like she was.

Bob: Yeah.

Bonnie: Cause that's how she came to Him. "Is this the Judgment Seat of Christ or the White Throne Judgment?"

Bob: You mean where did they go?

Bonnie: Yeah.

Bob: Uh, the second that He asked them a question they answered and the judgment was over.

Bonnie: So He's the White Throne Judgment?

Bob: I don't understand all this but their place in heaven is determined by how they answered Him. There was no other judgment for them.

Bonnie: I was thinking the other day about the Judgment Seat of Christ and the White Throne Judgment. So one is for the sinner (*Bob confirms*) and one is for the saved?

Bob: Yeah, well as you came to that Light, it was all there. You could not lie so I guess you could call it a judgment. But I'd call it Love.

So He asked that little eleven-year-old girl, "Did you learn to love?" And she said, "Oh, yes, Lord" for she couldn't have lied. You can't lie there. It wasn't her lips that was speaking it was her conscience, her spirit man. Then He reached out and embraced her and kissed her and in she went. And it was like this was one of the greatest testimonies that will be there.

Then in front of me was a woman that had died at ninety-three. Her fingers were nothing but huge knots. Arthritis had so attacked her body and hands for, I would say, fifty years and she had lived in great pain with arthritis. Then He asked her, "Did you learn to love?" And she said, "Only you Lord, I lost my husband young and I got bitter. I stayed in the church but I never really did anything but bite people because of my bitterness." But she wasn't in love and He told her, "You're saved by grace but in heaven you have no rewards. You'll be the least in the kingdom of heaven because you didn't learn to love." So in she went and I was next.

Bonnie: So, she only learned to love Him but not anyone else?

Bob: Yep. Her sin was that she should have learned to love others through Him. But she did love Him and she stayed in church all of her life.

Bonnie: So, the Lord asked the black woman and the little girl the same question, "Did you learn to Love? And the black woman responded with "Yes, Lord." Right? So she had great joy....

Bob: She responded with "Oh, Yes Lord." I mean she had a joy in Him. Her arms went up and there was great reward waiting for her. And the little eleven-year-old girl, as far as I could see everyone in that line, there was no greater reward for any of them but for her. She had fulfilled her ministry at eleven years old. Totally paralyzed at eleven but had finished her time and she was sure faithful in it.

Bonnie: Ok and now there's Bob.

Bob: I'm thinking, "Lord, I did get saved. I learned to love. I was doing what I was doing because I did love. And I was obeying You because I loved. I'm ready for my kiss." I'm puckered up. "And I won't have to ever go through pain again. I'll never have a bummer day again. This is the greatest day of my life." As I drew close to Him He looked at me with those blue eyes, which looked right through me. You talk about a spooky feeling; man, I mean He looked all over you. He could just look and instantly He x-rayed everything in you. I'm telling you, that was frightening. When the eye of God is on you, and I don't hear many people talking about it, but man it terrorized me!

Bonnie: So, are you the only person in line at this point?

Bob: Well, there were many behind me.

Bonnie: Well, yeah, but there's no one in front of you (*Bob confirms*) so you're the…

Bob: Yeah it was my time in line.

Bonnie: Since you're there now, describe more in detail what you saw.

Bob: Well, I saw this beautiful, beautiful white man and He was white light. And the only things that weren't white light were His two beautiful eyes. They were blue like two wells of blue water with light at the bottom. They were like two wells with the light shining and a depth that you could not see. You could not fathom the depth of it and they looked right through me. You couldn't hide anything from them. So then He put out His left hand and He said, "Satan has killed you before your time. I want you to go back because you were doing what I told you to do." And I'm thinking, your thoughts are really words there because your mouth isn't speaking.

Bonnie: Yeah, it's only your spirit speaking.

Bob: Yeah, and in my spirit I said, "I've not accomplished anything. I'm really failing." He said, "You're a liar because you brought My words and My words will accomplish the things I've sent them to do. You did obey Me in bringing them." Well, I didn't do very well on that one. And I said, "But it's so painful down there. I'm continually under persecution." And He said, "Yeah, your old nature was cowardly. That's the coward in you."

Bonnie: That was the coward in you speaking?

Bob: Yup. And He said, "But I will bring you in if you'll look at this line over here and turn your face back to Me for I want you to go back." So I turned my eyes toward the line and it was the most pitiful, horrible thing I've ever seen. So I turned back to Him and I said, "Lord, when I was saved in the Baptist Church I had this love for souls. I would go back for one soul. I would go back down and bear my cross for one soul."

He said, "I'm not sending you back to die for one soul. I'm sending you back to prepare the people for the greatest harvest of all time. I'm going to glorify Myself beyond anything man can imagine. And I'm going to bring over a billion youth into one great awakening. I want you to go back and speak to some of the leaders. I want you to tell them about Heaven and Hell. I want you to wake them up and support them. When you were a Baptist your main heart was leading someone to Me. Now I want you to go back and reveal Me to My leaders." I said, "OK." Then I got my kiss and the next thing you know I'm back in the room.

III
RETURN FROM DEATH

Love is sacrifice; love is gain.
Love is unknown and often has no name.
Love is childhood memories, forgetting the pain.
Its' bearing our cross and giving Him our shame.
Love is tomorrow, today and forever.

Bonnie: OK. So, now you're back in bed?

Bob: No. I wasn't in bed. I went back and I saw myself lying there in bed and that wet towel was still around me.

Bonnie: Oh, OK. So it's your spirit that was back.

Bob: Yes, the spirit of life.

Lyn: I was going to ask when you came back did you go back through the tunnel.

Bob: No I was back instantly.

Lyn: It was more like you blinked.

Bob: Yeah, BOOM! I didn't go back through the tunnel. I was just back. It was like a streak of lightning!

Bonnie: So you see yourself in the bed with the towel wrapped around your head, right?

Bob: Yeah a wet towel wrapped around my head and it was really bloody to where it would come out of my mouth. Then I looked and I could see the demon that had touched me. You know a lot of times you see a death spirit like a demon. Well that's exactly how they look. You know all those people's imaginations about a death spirit? They aren't wrong. He really looks like that.

Lyn: You mean like the grim reaper type thing?

Bob: Yeah and there were two angels that had literally shoved him back out of my way.

Bonnie: So, these are the two resurrection angels?

Bob: Well, yes. I didn't know it then but I do now.

Bonnie: What did the demon look like? Describe like how tall or thin or fat or…

Bob: Well, I would say that he was six foot six. And he was thin but he looked like a death spirit.

Bonnie: So he's all black and more like a shadow type thing?

Bob: He's covered in black. He had a black hood on just like people have pictured him. He looked just like that. I mean people that described him really got the right details of it. Now I saw him and I saw these two resurrection angels. The two angels were protecting me. Then when I looked back at him, he left. He was gone. Then I was thinking, I don't really want to go back in there (*my body*) but when I go back in there I'll be healed.

Lyn: Now, you said it was like the angels just pushed him back.

Bob: Yeah, they had total authority there over death.

Bonnie: OK, so the setting is the room…your bedroom…your body is in the bed but your, like, above it? (*Bob confirms*) So, you see the demon and you see the two angels (*Bob confirms*) and the angels push him out of the way but you still had a choice, at that time, to go back in your body. (*Bob confirms statements*). Because you thought you were going to be healed?

Bob: Well, I thought I was healed. And I was thinking, "Man, I'll go back in this body and we'll start the million soul harvest tomorrow."

Bonnie: I would probably think the same thing too. Let's get it going.

Bob: Yeah, man, I'm going back and now comes power evangelism and I'll see people coming to the Lord by the millions.

Lyn: You know, I got saved and that was fifteen or so years ago. I was sure I was one of the last…you know in the Lamb's Book of Life and probably right before "THE END" and now it's like fifteen years later.

Bonnie: We all must think that.

Bob: That's how I felt…you know like within a year they'll be a billion people come in and then the Lord will come.

Bob: So the body began to pull me towards it.

Bonnie: Ok so your body pulled you towards it?

Bob: Yeah, and I really wasn't all that hot getting back in it but

I was pulled back into it. Then I really got a shock. I went back into the pain. I wasn't healed. I couldn't understand it. I had just been standing before Jesus and I'd come back and I was really hurting bad.

Bonnie: OK, let's see, Wayne and Viola are somewhere in the house but how long do you feel that you were gone from your body? Minutes? Hours?

Bob: I'd say I died at three o'clock. And I'd say I come back in my body at 3 o'clock.

Bonnie: Oh, so everything was instantaneous?

Bob: Yeah, instantaneous.

Bonnie: And Viola and Wayne were outside the room?

Bob: Yeah, well they were coming in at different times.

Bonnie: But they don't know that you had this experience at that point?

Bob: Uh, no they don't. They didn't know until I came back. Then I told them.

Bonnie: Okay, and you think, all this took place like around three o'clock?

Bob: Oh, I came back at three o'clock. I know because when you come back you look. (*Meaning look at the clock*) I was back in my body and the pain was so horrible and I couldn't understand it. I said, "Lord, I came back so I know I'm not going to die." So, something had happened inside my mind. I heard a phone ring. Then I heard a voice talking to another voice I know saying, "Bob Jones is really sick so begin to pray for him."

So, Viola had called people to get them to pray for me. As they started praying for me I could hear their prayers. As they prayed my pain lessened. Then they would hang up from one another and call up some others and people began to pray for me all around. As they were praying for me my pain would let up. And that was a Friday.

So by Friday evening I wasn't feeling too bad. I couldn't eat anything yet because I was too sick but I was feeling pretty good. Some of the saints came over and laid hands on me. I was not feeling bad at all and then they left and I thought I could get some sleep. Although it was like pain literally kept me awake. Finally I couldn't hear them praying for me and then eventually the last person quit praying for me about five o'clock in the morning. And I'm thinking, "Oh, its sure going to be horrible until somebody starts praying for me again."

Now, the pain was returning full force. Not only could I hear but I had an open vision of an older woman, probably about fifty, that did office work early in the morning. She'd set her alarm a couple hours early and get up to pray for me. I saw her go down on her knees and begin to pray for me and then I went to sleep. Now this older lady usually sat at the back of the church 'caus she didn't take as many baths as the church thought she should have and her clothes weren't immaculate. But I sure found out something. Don't judge the saints because she prayed for me until she went to work. And when she went to work, others began to pray for me.

So, on Saturday saints came over and were praying for me again and I wasn't feeling bad. So, they asked me a question. They said, "Are you coming to church tomorrow?" Now the pain had lessened so I told them, "Yeah, I'll be there at the 10:30 service."

Bonnie: Saturday people came and prayed with you so were you still not able to get out of bed?

Bob: No, I couldn't get out of bed.

Bonnie: Were you able to eat or anything?

Bob: No I don't even think I could drink water. I may have but I don't remember.

Bonnie: So you couldn't eat and couldn't walk, but had the bleeding stopped?

Bob: Yep, the bleeding stopped when I came back in the body.

Lyn: The church that you were going to speak at on Sunday was it the same one you had spoken at a couple of days before?

Bob: Yeah! When they all left my house I could hear people in many different places praying for me. I didn't feel too bad but I wasn't resting any. So, the next morning (*Sunday*) the sister that had prayed for me before was now getting ready to go to church. The worst time I had ever seen was Sunday morning. There was no prayer for me, there was no prayer going up. Everyone was so busy getting ready for church they weren't praying. So really the darkest time that I saw, and I think that the darkest time right now is a Sunday morning.

Bob: Viola came in a couple of times and said, "Are you going to be able to go?" And I said, "No, look at me I'm swelled up worse." Boy, I was really swollen. "I'm worse. I can't even move now."

Bonnie: So, this was Sunday, August 10th? (*Bob confirms*)

Bob: And fifteen after ten, wham! Everything was gone. I could get out of bed.

Bonnie: Sure, you were going to the ten-thirty service.

Bob: Yeah, I got out of bed and went to the bathroom. Man what passed out of me was like green slime. I would say that the green slime was like old blood. It just poured out of me and I told Viola, "We're going." And we went to the ten-thirty service and I gave testimony on it.

Bonnie: You hadn't been out of bed for two days and now at ten-fifteen Sunday morning, what happened?

Bob: Everything was gone.

Bonnie: Were you praying?

Bob: My whole body could move.

Lyn: Your stomach's swelling must have gone down.

Bob: Yeah, well it hadn't gone down until I went to the bathroom.

Lyn: Oh, OK.

Bonnie: But did you pray like, "God, You've got to heal me?"

Bob: Uh no. I was hurting too bad. When you hurt that bad sometimes you live a half second at a time. You live from one second to another or one minute to another or one hour to another. You watch the clock.

Bonnie: OK so then at ten-fifteen everything was just healed in that moment?

Bob: Everything became normal. So I've always said I'll never put a limit on God when I'm going to do a thing. I should have told them I was going to be at the Sunday morning nine-thirty service. I really think that I put the word on me. I spoke by faith so I said ten-thirty.....I should have said, "Yes, I'll be there. I'll be all right!

Bonnie: Now that green substance – was it just urine? You didn't have anything else like vomiting?

Bob: Just green slime stuff that took about three days to pass through.

Bonnie: Ok well, let's go back to before you go to church. It's ten-fifteen and everything is healed. And you feel normal so you get up and pee…

Bob: Everything's been lifted off me. I don't know how to describe it but it's like a ton of weight was on me and now it was gone!

Bonnie: Ok, so, now you go to church (*Bob confirms*) at the ten-thirty service. How did the people react? Were they excited or surprised to see you?

Bob: Just a few, those that prayed for me where glad to see me. But many that prayed for me weren't in church. They had left the church. (*Bob meant they left after the earlier service*)

Bonnie: Ok, but were these the ones there that you had talked to Friday night at the church?

Bob: They were at another church. See they weren't where I was. Some of them were pastors at their own church, pastors of small flocks. The one person that was there was that sister sitting on the back row with her shabby clothes. She had a friend for life.

Bonnie: So, the people that are at the church this Sunday morning are not the same people that were at the church when you… (*Bob interrupts*)

Bob: No. There were, maybe, five or six people that came over and prayed for me from this church.

Bonnie: Did you get up and give testimony that day? (*Bob confirms*) and you told them all that happened? (*Bob confirms*) And how did they respond? This is your testimony.

Bob: They didn't believe me.

Bonnie: Imagine that. So you told them and they didn't believe you?

Bob: Yep, and so a few months after that they threw me out.

Bonnie: Well, we better get a little more detail about that day though. Seriously, you go to the church and there are only five or six people there that really…

Bob: Well, one of 'em was Viola's nephew's family. They all went to praying for me. They were there that day. And they were running around, especially the children, running around saying, "God has healed Uncle Bob." So they were all excited.

Bonnie: What was your relationship with the pastor? Did he know that you were sick and did he come out to pray for you or not?

Bob: Ah yeah, he did but he didn't. (*He was aware of Bob's illness but didn't come to the house to pray for him.*)

Bonnie: Ok so the pastor didn't come out to pray. Did he let you get up to give testimony that day?

Bob: Well, when you had something like that you could give it. So we had testimonies then. In the Baptist church testimonies are part of the service. So my problems just begin there.

Bonnie: So, it really wasn't a happy ending to that story, so to speak, as far as that church went?

Bob: Well, you can write a happy ending if you want to but it would be a lie.

Bonnie: No. I mean it wasn't well received in the church that day.

Bob: No, but those that heard did. I'd say ten percent of the people there heard my testimony. Then the rest of them didn't believe what I was saying was right. It wasn't a near death experience for me. It was a death experience. It wasn't near.

Bonnie: Let me go back to something. When you were sent back and you're in your room and see your body. Then, you said, your body drew your spirit back into it…

Bob: Like I didn't have a choice, like you're being funneled right back into your body.

Did You Learn To Love?

Bonnie: Did you take a big breath?

Bob: Uh, I don't know. I only know I started breathing and unwrapped the thing around my head. I didn't get out of bed but I took the bloody towel off my head.

Bonnie: And when you were in heaven and you were with the Holy Spirit did you just… walk or glide?

Bob: Uh, well, you don't walk like you do here.

Bonnie: So it was more like you glide?

Bob: I guess you might say that.

Bonnie to Lyn: Is there anything else you'd like to ask?

Lyn: Yeah, I'll probably think of stuff later.

Bob: Yeah, that's my testimony and I'm going to stick to it. You got one minute to clear the deck.

Lyn: When you were up there with Jesus, you were facing Jesus?

Bob: We all will face Him.

Lyn: What was the background? What did it look like? Was it like clouds?

Bob: You mean behind Him?

Lyn: Yes, like were there clouds or…

Bob: Ah, no there was light. The light of all lights radiated from Him, an inner glowing. He was the light all the way back. In both lines we saw the light. He is a Light. He is a brighter light than can be bright but it doesn't hurt you. He is the most beautiful person I've ever seen. And every picture they have of Him, you know people hanging over Him? Well that's not Him.

Bonnie: When you were the first one in line going toward Him, did you see His eyes? Or was He just light? Did He have features like we do?

Bob: He had all the features of a man.

Lyn: But it was all light?

Bob: But it was all light; different colors of light and it was all white. The most beautiful white light I've ever seen. But it was also a love light. It was also a glory light. You felt loved and you felt so secure in His light. But that other line they saw the light for the last time.

Bonnie: Did you hear any sounds or anything? Was there anything significant? Did you hear anything besides the voice of the Holy Spirit or the voice of Jesus or the people that were screaming?

Bob: I heard the voice of the saints as they would say 'yes' and I heard the moaning and groaning and screaming of those that were going down into eternal darkness. But that was so horrible I didn't want to look at it.

Bonnie: But there was no noise, like we would have in the natural; like you hear the train or birds or the clock ticking?

Bob: No, no, no! I didn't hear any of that. No birds. No nothing.

Bonnie: Any other questions?

Lyn: No

Bonnie: Thank you Mr. Bob. Thank you for giving us a closer look at your death experience from August 8, 1975.

Bob: I'm ready for my Cornish hens

IV

HOW CAN I LEARN TO LOVE?

Love is the Keeper of the keys.
Love meets you on bended knees.
Love sees through all impossibilities,
and brings hope and stability.

Many people may wonder what does it mean to love or how can I learn to love? It's a valid question. How does one learn to love? We are born into a fallen state; a world full of wickedness and shame, discouragement and unbelief. There are rules to follow every way you turn and many raise an eyebrow or wear scorn on their face. It's a fast paced rat race out there and no one seems to stop and take time for his or her fellow man. How can you learn to love when the world is so full of panic and unbelief?

It is true we are born into a fallen state surrounded by the haste of the world and the antics of the enemy. However, when we begin our journey with the Lord by saying "yes" to His invitation to eternal life, we begin a relationship of love. It includes our journey of trust and obedience, humility and honor, peace and joy.

We begin to see the world through different eyes and with different values. Instead of seeing people as they are, we see them as God does. Each one is a unique individual formed from eternity past and sent to reside on the earth at God's destined time in history. No two people's DNA is the same yet each one carries God's DNA when they are born again. When we're born again there's a transformation that takes place within our spirit man and a renewing of our mind. Therefore we begin looking at others through the eyes of God, instead of our natural eyes. Instead of seeing the rugged and scorned person that has been steeped in sin we see the blessed child of God whom He has called His beloved.

Trust Is Part Of Love's Equation

Trust plays a major role. How can we trust a God that we can't even see? How do we know He hears us and if He does, will He answer us? Trust is part of love's equation. Remember God loved us first not the other way around. Therefore He trusted us and called us to be His own. In turn we trust Him with our lives when we accept Christ as our Savior. Love and trust go hand in hand. The more we trust God the more we love Him. And the more we love Him the more we trust Him. He on the other hand cannot love us anymore because He has already demonstrated all of His love on the cross. Of course, we may at times feel His love in a greater measure because things seem to work out for our good to a greater degree. However we have the maximum of His love poured out to us at all times. In the same way the fullness of His trust is always available to us, however in our immaturity we don't recognize it. As we grow into a greater measure of His love by demonstration toward the saints, we develop a greater measure of His trust. The greatest measure of man's love is that he'd lay down his life for his brother.

"Greater love has no one than this, than to lay down one's life for his friends." **(John 15:13)**

Compassionate Love

I'm going to share something that the Lord gave me several years ago. I'm quoting what the Lord Jesus spoke to me that gave me an understanding of how faith works by love.

"There is a love so deep man has never explored, but in this season the Father will begin to teach you how to love the unlovely and those who betray you. You will learn to love back to life those who are dying by natural and spiritual deaths. There are many ways to love your brother and in this season the Father will teach you compassionate love. And you must display Jesus' love from the cross."

There is a deeper compassion man has never understood. The Father taught Me this that day as I hung there naked. Although they mocked and spit upon Me while I was on the cross, I looked at them with love. The love of the Father is without condemnation because it is with full acceptance of the sinner's sin. He loves them with the love of His Son that was worked in Me that day.

No greater love has man than he'd give his life for his brother. That was the greatest testing of My faith. To walk in the faith of God you must know this and demonstrate it daily. Choose to love all mankind no matter what their sin. Just love them! You cannot stray from the cross. It is the final crucifying of the flesh. Love God, love yourself and love your brother."

Although Jesus was mocked and spit upon during His crucifixion, He returned love for their evil deeds. He lay down His life voluntarily for His brother; all mankind. **(John 10:17-18)** This was the greatest testing of Jesus' faith.

Should the measure of our love be less? Is it possible to love and forgive to the same degree Jesus did on that great and terrible day of His crucifixion? I believe it is. Once we are born again, our whole being is in Him. He is our life, our death and our resurrection. He is our all in all. There is no beginning or end to the depths of His love nature. And we were created in His divine image "love." How can we be any different unless we choose to be? If we walk in His light guided by the Holy Spirit then we mature in the nine fruits of the Spirit. **(Galatians 5:22-23)** The first fruit mentioned is "love" because all things begin and end with love (God).

Can you imagine the faith, love and forgiveness that were worked in Mary's heart that day? Knowing that she birthed the Son of God and watched over Him all the days of His life, now she must surrender her final will unto the Father. It was the last crucifying of her heart. Although Mary's heart was being gripped with agony for her Son, still joy arose within her knowing He was completing the Father's will for all mankind. She also had to forgive those who crucified her Son and receive the gift of love from her new son, John the beloved. In his own words, he was the one Jesus loved. I believe John had the greatest understanding of Jesus' compassionate love. That's why Jesus trusted His beloved mother to John's care.

Now there stood by the cross of Jesus His mother, and His mother's sister, Mary the wife of Clopas, and Mary Magdalene. When Jesus therefore saw His mother, and the disciple whom He loved standing by, He said to His mother, "Woman, behold your son!" Then He said to the disciple, "Behold your mother!" And from that hour that disciple took her to his own home. **(John 19:25-27)**

A true act of love will disarm the enemy and render him defenseless. It's a choice we make by the words we speak. The only authority Satan has is empowered by words. Our words of love will starve the devil and weaken his defenses. Satan thought the victory was his when he convinced man to kill the Son of God. But when Jesus said, "Forgive them Father," He released power into the earth. In the same way, when you truly forgive and choose to love, you release the same kingdom power and the enemy has no defense against it. Satan cannot combat it. That's why love is such a powerful weapon in the mouths of the saints.

"And when they had come to the place called Calvary, there they crucified Him, and the criminals, one on the right hand and the other on the left. Then Jesus said, "Father, forgive them, for they do not know what they do." **(Luke 23:33-34)**

Love Leads to Obedience

Love is like oil to the wheels of obedience. It enables us to run the way of God's commandment to love. **(Romans 13:8-10)** When we come to the realization of the Father's love for an unforgiving world and the fact He gave His only Son as sacrifice for our sin, His love will overwhelm us. Out of our longing for intimacy with the Father, we desire to be obedient and walk the way of the cross. From that place of intimacy, God positions us to receive His love unhindered, free flowing and full of power.

"Owe no one anything except to love one another, for he who loves another has fulfilled the law. For the commandments, "You

shall not commit adultery," "You shall not murder," "You shall not steal," "You shall not bear false witness," "You shall not covet," and if there is any other commandment, are all summed up in this saying, namely, "You shall love your neighbor as yourself." Love does no harm to a neighbor; therefore love is the fulfillment of the law." **(Romans 13:8-10)**

It's like an umbilical cord; everything you receive is straight from the Father; pure without interference. The more intimate you are with the Him, the more you desire His will in all aspects of your life. As you become more Christ centered and lay your agendas down you'll desire His will no matter what the cost in the natural. This is what Jesus did. He willingly went to the cross, He chose the Father's will not His own. There was no darkness in Him; Satan had no point of entry.

"I will not talk with you much more, for the prince (evil genius, ruler) of the world is coming. And he has no claim on Me. [He has nothing in common with Me; there is nothing in Me that belongs to him, and he has no power over Me.] But [Satan is coming and] I do as the Father has commanded Me, so that the world may know (be convinced) that I love the Father and that I do only what the Father has instructed Me to do. [I act in full agreement with His orders.] Rise, let us go away from here." **(John 14:30&31 Amplified)**

There is a body of believers that is now moving into that place of total intimacy with the Father and they are consumed by the presence of God. It's a place of total surrender and there the enemy will be unable to find a place in them. They will walk in the power and demonstration of the kingdom as it was in the beginning. God's word is creative and full of power. It is without hindrance and has no restrictions. It is full of force; He has given us all authority.

The woes of this world; fear, infirmities, sorrow, torment, plagues, poverty etc., have no hold on us. We have been set free by the blood of Jesus and seated in heavenly places. We are not bound by the woes of this world but loosed into the glory and splendor of His light, power, knowledge, understanding and wisdom.

LOVE IS THE UNIVERSAL KEY

Love often challenges and
Makes you grow stronger
Love is a tapestry of art,
God's workmanship; His heart.

Love is the universal key that unlocks the heart of mankind and brings, solemnly, home the lost and forbidden. Love is the greatest tool to salvation. It's a language that needs no words. It's the heartbeat of the Father leaning toward His children that brings a longing in their heart to cling to His robe. Love is never ending!

Not everything we do in life seems pleasant to our flesh. Sometimes we encounter unlikely situations that rub us the wrong way or they don't seem fair or right. Somehow it doesn't fit into our schedule or our way of thinking. At times we feel like life hasn't dealt us a very good hand. None of us are exempt from bad or difficult things happening in our life. One key to remember, that will help overcome difficult situations, is that in all things we do, do them as unto the Lord.

1 Corinthians 13

I Corinthians 13 is considered the love chapter because Paul eloquently describes the characteristics of the true nature of God. Christ is His Son and He demonstrated the fullness of His Father's nature. Now we are children of God and are called to walk in the same likeness of our Father and Brother. The way that we do this is to be a vessel of His love by following His life's pattern in these scriptures.

God is Love **(1 John 4:8)** and the whole essence of His being is love. I like the Amplified version of this chapter because it better describes what love is and what it is not.

4. *Love endures long and is patient and kind; love never is envious nor boils over with jealousy, is not boastful or vainglorious, does not display itself haughtily.*

5. *It is not conceited (arrogant and inflated with pride); it is not rude (unmannerly) and does not act unbecomingly. Love (God's love in us) does not insist on its own rights or its own way, for it is not self-seeking; it is not touchy or fretful or resentful; it takes no account of the evil done to it [it pays no attention to a suffered wrong].*

6. *It does not rejoice at injustice and unrighteousness, but rejoices when right and truth prevail.*

7. *Love bears up under anything and everything that comes, is ever ready to believe the best of every person, its hopes are fadeless under all circumstances, and it endures everything [without weakening].*

8. *Love never fails [never fades out or becomes obsolete or comes to an end].* **(1 Corinthians 13:4-8a)**

It's important we remember that when we stand in front of Jesus there's only one question He'll ask each one of us. We won't have time to conjure up some lame excuse or think about what we should have done. We are spirit to spirit with the Holy Son of God and our spirit can't lie. We might have labored hard and accomplished extraordinary deeds or performed many acts of valor but if we have not learned to be a vessel of His love to others, we have accomplished nothing.

"We can have great faith and demonstrate the miraculous but if we have not love, we are nothing." **(1 Corinthians 13:2)**

Love is Forgiveness

Love means forgiving no matter what the circumstance. Forgive! If we don't forgive others – God can't forgive us.

"But if you do not forgive men their trespasses, neither will your Father forgive your trespasses." **(Matthew. 6:15)**

Unconditional love means not putting our demands or conditions on another – just love them. As the Father loves us with our sin nature so we must love our brother. Simply love the sinner and hate their sin.

Sacrificial love is to lay down your life for others; deny yourself and pick up your cross. God gave His only begotten Son to die for our sins. Jesus went to the cross by His own will.

Love your neighbor. Jesus said to him, *"'You shall love the Lord your God with all your heart, with all your soul, and with all your mind.' This is the first and great commandment. And the second is like it: 'You shall love your neighbor as yourself.' On these two commandments hang all the Law and the Prophets."* **(Matthew 22:37-40)**

Love your enemies. This is perhaps the most difficult testing of love but it is possible to do. When I was going through a very difficult time in my life the Father told me I had to love a certain person that was in the process of destroying my character. Of course, I gave the Lord reasons why it was impossible for me to love this person. Again He told me that I must love this person and again I answered I can't! Then the Father gently said to me that I must love this person the same way He loved those who crucified His Son. I deeply repented for my hardness of heart and stubborn behavior. The Lord taught me that my love for the Lord is far greater than any degree of hurt or offense anyone can bring against me. I must remember it's not the person; it's an anti-Christ spirit operating in the other person. We do not war against flesh and blood.

"But I say to you who hear: Love your enemies, do good to those who hate you, bless those who curse you, and pray for those who spitefully use you. To him who strikes you on the one cheek, offer the other also. And from him who takes away your cloak, do not withhold your tunic either. Give to everyone who asks of you. And from him who takes away your goods do not ask them back." **(Luke 6:27-30)**

We have the ability within us to turn our conversation into intercession. Instead of gossiping about someone who treats you unkindly, pray for him or her. See them through the Father's eyes of love and speak life, love and His destiny into them. Begin to treat them according to the "golden rule" after all, isn't that the way you would want them to treat you?

"And just as you want men to do to you, you also do to them likewise." **(Luke 6:31)**

No Fear in Love

There is no fear in love. Why? Because God is Love and He loved us first and called us to be His own. He is in us and we are in Him. As we continue to grow in "His love" we develop a more perfect love. Love toward Him, toward our self and for our brethren.

A mature or perfect love casts out fear and lives by faith and hope in Christ as they're lead by the Holy Spirit of Truth. Fear cannot dwell in a mature vessel of love. Fear brings with it terror, despair, anxiety and hopelessness. Fear knows no love.

"There is no fear in love [dread does not exist], but full-grown (complete, perfect) love turns fear out of doors and expels every trace of terror! For fear brings with it the thought of punishment, and [so] he who is afraid has not reached the full maturity of love [is not yet grown into love's complete perfection]. We love Him, because He first loved us." **(1 John 4:18-19 Amplified)**

Too many times I've heard Christians say they cannot forgive another person because of something they said or did against them. Sometimes it's an old family matter that's never been resolved and over the years it has festered in their souls. It's often an ex-mate or parent that's so wounded them they find it impossible to forgive them. Most commonly the hurt, wound, deception or whatever you might want to call it comes from someone we loved and trusted. The hurt goes so deep and without forgiveness bitterness sets in. Yet these wounded souls are good Christians and attend church every Sunday without fail and many hold positions in the church. They really have a love for the Lord and you can see their fruit. But the reality is they hate their brother or the one that wounded them. Therefore they are not perfected vessels of love and their fruit is tainted. If anyone says he loves God but hates his brother, he is a liar.

"If anyone says, I love God, and hates (detests, abominates) his brother [in Christ], he is a liar; for he who does not love his brother, whom he has seen, cannot love God, Whom he has not seen." **(1 John 4:20 Amplified)**

How do we change this? Love your brother. Forgive him and love him. It doesn't mean you have to trust him again but we are commanded to love. Love is our DNA.

"And this command (charge, order, and injunction) we have from Him: that he who loves God shall love his brother [believer] also." **(1 John 4:21 Amplified)**

The enemy has no weapon against love and therefore he'll continue adding salt to the wound as a constant reminder of the hurt or offense. Each time you rehash the incident it adds fuel to his flame and draws you farther away from perfected love in Christ. It takes an act of love to forgive from your heart. But when you do, you release your weapon of love and the enemy has no defense against it. He's the defeated foe and you draw nearer to God.

VI
PREFERRING OTHERS FIRST

Love knows no depth, no height, in its' shadows only delight. Love is timeless, it is narrow. Love is inescapable. Love bears up its' brother.

Preferring Others First

Now you might ask, "What does this mean?" In this day and age we tend to see selfish, self-centered people around the globe. Its' a dog eat dog world and everybody is out to get what they can for themselves. Rarely do people prefer others first. But let's take a look at Jesus' ministry and how He became a servant to His chosen disciples. On the night He was betrayed, the Master Himself, became servant and washed the disciple's feet. Christ preferred mankind and offered Himself up as our sacrificial Lamb.

Preferring others first is an act of love. It's simply putting other's needs ahead of your own. Another way to put it is – acts of kindness. Our heart should be overjoyed with love when we can help another achieve their destiny. It can be as simple as giving up your seat on the bus or subway; or perhaps shoveling a neighbor's driveway, cooking a meal for a shut in or just spending time with the elderly. Sometimes it's the smallest insignificant things that will make a great difference in someone else's life. Preferring others first is stepping aside and allowing another to shine brighter than you. Remember, God looks at our heart not our outward deeds. Many things we do for others will go unnoticed by man but God does not overlook it.

I'm reminded of the ninety-three year old woman that was ahead of Bob in the line. She was crippled from arthritis because of the bitterness of her heart. Although she learned to love the Lord she didn't love anyone else. She became acquainted with His love and knew His kindness, compassion, peace and joy yet she chose not to love others as He loved her.

She basically spent a lifetime of knowing His love and not sharing it, kind of like the man that hid the talents. **(Matthew 25)** Love is the expression of Christ operating through us toward others.

The Father granted me opportunity to witness Bob's departure from this life to eternal life. In that process I observed many things; I came to understand how Bob so loved the Lord, and the body of Christ, that he would choose the Father's will over his own in order to complete all that he was called to do on earth. Nine days prior to Bob's departure he was very near death in the emergency room. Two large resurrection angels came to escort him home. Bob told me that he had double lights on his eyes and was up the stairs and standing at the door. It was at this point Bob could make a choice to enter eternity or remain and continue the Father's will. Although three doctors urged me to sign release forms so they wouldn't treat him and allow him to die, I couldn't make that decision. Bob would know when his work on earth was done.

In the days that followed leading up to the morning of Valentine's Day I observed many supernatural things taking place with Bob. On that last night, he was once again up the stairs and this time trying to get to the door. Satan himself stood between Bob and Heaven's door to oppose his entry. What seemed so easy just nine days ago was now a work of love. We worked together to combat the opposing force and displace the enemy. Bob had many messages yet to deliver that morning before he went home to the Father. I'm proud to say that I know Bob finished well and completed all that he was sent to do on this earth. He could have taken the easy way out and given up early, but his love for the Father and the body were so great that he gave it all until his last breath.

It's our sacrifice of walking in faith that gives opportunity for others to advance. This was a true demonstration of how faith works by love. Bob's love energized his faith that propelled him to continue no matter the cost. His physical body was wasted. There was no strength left in him yet his spirit man arose and completed the task at hand.

I witnessed firsthand **John 15:13**, Greater love has no one than this, than to lay down one's life for his friends. When we prefer others first, we place their needs above our own. Bob's life was dedicated to see the body of Christ advance to the fullness of its potential in the Spirit. I believe that in the days before his death it became more intense because the devil knew his time was short and he was trying to rob the body. But Bob fought the good fight and warred with Satan and defeated him time after time. And the body of Christ is better because of God's love worked through Bob.

VII
CREATED IN HIS LOVE

There is no time in love.
It is without beginning
It is without end
Love is eternal
Love is your Friend.

Over two thousand years ago mankind received the revelation of the Son of God when the Word became flesh and dwelled among men. That sperm seed was sent from the Father by the Holy Spirit to become the Christ child born of a virgin in the fullness of time.

"And the Word became flesh and dwelt among us, and we beheld His glory, the glory as of the only begotten of the Father, full of grace and truth." **(John 1:14)**

Love is the seed from the Father and the Father is Love. All mankind comes from the seed of the Father. **(Genesis 1:26-28)** *"God said 'Let Us make man in Our image.' So in the image of God He created him; male and female He created them."* All mankind begins as a seed that fertilizes an egg to become a living being inside the womb of woman. Each infant that is born is born out of that seed of love and unknowingly loves unconditionally. A child's heart is pure or you could say their soul is uncorrupted.

For years I have heard people say that babies are born selfish but I tend to disagree. Babies come from the presence of God and their whole being is love centered. Think what a shock it is to a newborn baby entering a world of wickedness. Now this baby must adjust to a new atmosphere of breathing contaminated air, extreme light, noise and temperatures; whereas their place of intimacy with the Father and the presence of His love were pure. When man dies, his seed returns to the Father, if he was born again.

"At times you might feel left out or all alone. Remember, the Father's love is always available if you have accepted His offer of a saving relationship with His Son. There is nothing more fulfilling or meaningful than experiencing His divine affection. Draw near to God, and let Him fill your heart with His perfect love." - **Bob Jones**

There is no such thing as a mistaken or unwanted baby because all babies are a gift from God. Each one of us is a creation of God's and created in His image of Love. They are not unwanted because God desires that each one serve Him in His kingdom. Each one has been kissed with a kiss of joy and laughter and placed gently in the womb. Then the Father waits patiently for the time they mature and return to Him in the likeness of His Son Jesus Christ.

Every human being has had the same experience. Each one came from being in the presence of God, where we dwelled in the presence of His majesty and beheld the magnificence of His power. Although babies enter this life unable to verbalize, they live in the wonderment of God while being transitioned into the world. Because they have just left His presence, if they could speak from birth they would tell of His love, glory and the mysteries of the ages.

The Circle of Life

God is eternal; He has no beginning or end and is not bound by time. Jesus, the Lamb of God, was slain from the foundation of the world. **(Revelation 13:8)** In natural time, this took place at the end of His life on earth. When His mission on earth was complete He would be crucified, entombed, resurrected and ascend to Heaven. Yet in eternity it had already taken place before the foundation of the world.

And all the inhabitants of the earth will fall down in adoration and pay him homage, everyone whose name has not been recorded in the Book of Life of the Lamb that was slain [in sacrifice] from the foundation of the world. **(Revelation 13:8 Amplified)**

Since God is eternal and we were made in His image **(Genesis 1:26)** it is part of our divine inheritance in Christ to live in the eternal realm also. I believe that, like Christ, we have already lived our life in the spirit realm. All that we have done or will ever do has already been done in eternity past. At conception it becomes part of our DNA in eternity present. The "time" we occupy on earth we spend reconnecting or communing with the Father who sent us. It is in this place we are seeking Him for His perfect will for our life. I believe we are seeking the path that we have already traveled in eternity past. The Father requires an account of what we have done contrary to His divine outline for our lives. **(Ecclesiastes 3:15)** He has a divine plan and purpose for every being.

Jesus, the Perfect Lamb, understood eternity and His love for the Father was so strong that He would not stray from the path He had already taken. He would complete His work on the cross in demonstration of man's salvation. The Apostle Peter explains this truth in even more detail when he wrote about the precious blood of Christ.

"Knowing that you were not redeemed with corruptible things, like silver or gold, from your aimless conduct received by tradition from your fathers, but with the precious blood of Christ, as of a lamb without blemish and without spot. He indeed was foreordained before the foundation of the world, but was manifest in these last times for you." **(1 Peter 1:18-20)**

The reality is this. The blood of Jesus was shed for us before the creation of the world, but was only revealed to us when Jesus was crucified on the cross, died and rose again. Not even Satan knew about the shed blood until then. This truth, once understood, should have great implications for our faith and victorious living over Satan, sin and sickness.

Peter makes it clear (in verses 18 and 19 above) that we are "redeemed from the empty way of life by the blood of Christ" and that this was accomplished "before the creation of the world." In other words, the fall of mankind did not destroy God's purpose in creating mankind. It only restricted them to be bound by time.

I call this the circle of life. God is eternal and created us as eternal beings from eternity past and placed us in the womb of eternity present. This is where we become bound by time and limitations. There was no time before the fall so God created time for man not man for time. We begin in the presence of God like Jesus did and we're sent to earth to reconnect with the Father. Jesus lived in both realms, earthly and eternity. As a physical man He was bound by time yet as an eternal being He accessed the eternal realm of the Father. This is our inheritance as well. I believe that is where Bob lived or went a lot of times. He would say, "In that place that I go." I believe he understood the eternal realm although he couldn't put it into words. However the words he brought from "that place" were one hundred per cent accurate and his words never fell to the ground. I believe that when we get an understanding on this and begin to live in that eternal realm, we will experience the greater works.

Then Jesus answered and said to them, *"Most assuredly, I say to you, the Son can do nothing of Himself, but what He sees the Father do; for whatever He does, the Son also does in like manner. For the Father loves the Son, and shows Him all things that He Himself does; and He will show Him greater works than these, that you may marvel."* **(John 5:19-20)**

Our last phase of life is eternity future. If we are born again we spend eternity future with the Father in Heaven, which is eternal life and light. However, if we have not come to the knowledge of the Lord Jesus Christ our eternal future will be darkness.

All mankind will have a witness of the Son of God in their lifetime. They will each have opportunity to accept or reject Him. It's that simple. God loves us so much He'll even send multiple witnesses but it is always man's free will to choose.

These were the people in the line to the left that Bob spoke about in his death experience. As each one was heading into eternal darkness they saw the Son of God and recognized Him. They knew that they had been witnessed to, but selfish pride wouldn't let them accept Him as Lord and Savior. Now it was too late. We will all see Him face to face but for some it will be too late and they will spend all eternity with the gods they worshipped here. The gods they put before Him.

Bob told me one time about his visit to Hell. It was so gruesome and awful he didn't like to talk about it. The smell was horrible and the sounds of people calling out in agony were beyond words.

The Lord sent Bob to witness to a young man. He was young, handsome and a picture of health. He was successful in business and had a loving wife and three children and attended church. He seemed like your all American male. But he also had a wild side that included other women and alcohol. Bob witnessed to him once and then a second time. And the young man just laughed and shrugged it off. He was on top of the world, he had it all. A few months later Bob was told to go to this man again and tell him, "This is your last warning; for

I won't come to you again." This time the young man laughed all the louder and cussed at Bob and told him to get lost. About a week later this young man was killed in a car accident. Yes he was a picture of health and had all the material things he wanted but he didn't have Christ.

When Bob visited Hell he saw this young man. In fact he saw his head swinging in a macramé basket holder. And the young man continued crying out; "I should have listened to that old man!" Over and over again Bob saw his head swinging and heard him screaming but no one could help him or answer him now. Obviously he was an atheist and ultimately worshipped himself. As Bob recounted the line to the left, the thousand pound pumpkin head is atheist.

Summary

I'm thankful for the opportunity to share Bob's death experience and give you greater insight and revelation. Bob lived a supernatural lifestyle in the awe of God. It was his greatest pleasure to share his testimony. The Lord sent him back from death with a message for the saved as well as the unsaved. Hopefully the unsaved will consider the forsaken line and accept Christ into their lives. As for the saved, let them be an expression of God's love in action.

I love the way Bob told of the beauty and majesty of the Lord as He stood in line and beheld His glory, and how beautiful His eyes were. The amazing thing – when we stand in front of Him we are unable to speak. Our spirit does the talking and its all truth. The decision to love must be made before we leave this earthly body. We can only learn to love by accepting Christ as Lord and Savior. Once we've made that commitment, our desire is toward Him and we begin to love. Only through death to self and life in Him do we mature into a perfected love. Knowing His love is to know His will. Then we say, "Yes Lord, let it be according to Your will. I want Your will not mine."

It's the question that echoes out to all mankind for all eternity **"Did you learn to love?"**

"All the foundations of God are built on love. If you've learned to love, then you have obeyed everything God wants you to do. Love, He is our greatest pleasure. When you are in love with Jesus, He becomes your greatest pleasure." - **Bob Jones**

"And may the Lord make you increase and abound in love to one another and to all, just as we do to you, so that He may establish your hearts blameless in holiness before our God and Father at the coming of our Lord Jesus Christ with all His saints." ***(1 Thessalonians 3:12-13)***

PHOTO GALLERY

In this section I'd like to share with you some photos taken throughout Bob's time in ministry. It would be impossible to display photos of all of his friends and acquaintances. As you know Bob had friends all over the world. I've tried to select a few from Bob's earlier ministry as well as his later years. You will recog-nize the warmth of his smile and intensity in his eye of ministry.

Bob Ministering In Moravian Falls In 2001

Above – 2002 Bill & Beni Johnson with Mahesh & Bonnie Chavda celebrating Bob & Viola's 50th Anniversary.

Below – Bob & Viola In 2002

Right - Bob & Joe Cummings In Panama City Beach, Florida

Above -Paul Keith & Wanda Davis With Bob & Viola

Right – Bob teaching in August 2002

Left – Bob with little angels Joshua & Josiah Earl in October 1988.

Below - Bob & Viola And His Brother Roy & Norma J

Bob & Jane Aguilar

Bob Hartley with Bob & Bonnie in August 2008

Below Bob & Bonnie's Wedding Dance May 21, 2006

Right - Bob With Julie Earl Are Celebrating A Shared Birthday

Left - Bob In August 2008

Below - Jeff Jansen & Ryan Wyatt With Bob

Bob & Bonnie With Friend Gary Beaton

Bob With Ricky Skaggs In 2002

Left - Bobby & Carolyn Conner With Bob & Bonnie

Below - The Jones' Wedding Party. From Left To Right: Lyn Kost, Jacqueline Chappell, Bonnie Jones, Robin McMillan, Bob Jones, Elijah Chappell, Rick Joyner & Wayne Jones

Above - Bob in 2003

Left - Todd Bentley Sits Listening intently To Bob's Message At The Lakeland Florida Revival in 2008.

Bob With His Son Wayne Jones

Arthur Burt With Bob In July 2012

Carroll Henderson & Bob With Lyn & Katie Kost.

Robin McMillan With Bob Jones & Rick Joyner in May 2006

Family Photo July 2013 - Bob & Bonnie Jones Along With Lyn, Katie, Olivia & Avalyn Kost, and with Kimberly & Doug Glover, Mychal Volkert, Brandon & Jordan Gill.

Other Available Titles at www.bobjones.org

Poetry From the Heart

The Power of the Spoken Word

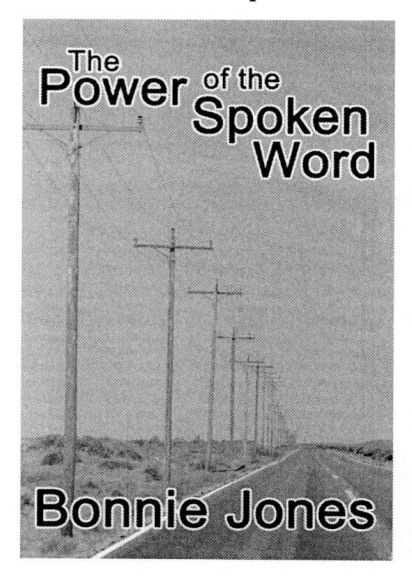

Shepherd's Rod 2015

Shepherd's Rod 2014

341	Fruit of the Spirit
341 The Kingdom of Heaven Series Bob & Bonnie Jones	Fruit of the Spirit The Kingdom of Heaven Series Bob & Bonnie Jones
Shepherd's Rod 2013	Shepherd's Rod 2012

Cover art created by *Lyn Kost*
(704)-975-9631
lyn@bobjones.org

To obtain more of Bob and Bonnie Jones' written, video and audio teachings, prophecies and materials go to www.BobJones.org

or write to:
      White Horses Publishing
      P.O. Box 838
      Pineville, N.C. 28134-0838